SMART WORDS
READER
BLIZZARDS
Christine A. Caputo
SCHOLASTIC INC.

What are SMART WORDS?

Smart Words are frequently used words that are critical to understanding concepts taught in the classroom. The more Smart Words a child knows, the more easily he or she will grasp important curriculum concepts. Smart Words Readers introduce these key words in a fun and motivational format while developing important literacy skills. Each new word is highlighted, defined in context, and reviewed. Engaging activities at the end of each chapter allow readers to practice the words they have learned.

ISBN 978-0-545-36822-3

Packaged by Q2AMedia

Picture Credit: t= top, b= bottom, l= left, r= right, c= center

Cover Page: Kordcom/Age fotostock/Photolibrary.
Title Page: László Gelesz/Istockphoto.
Content Page: Leonid_Tit/Shutterstock.

4-5: Gregor Kervina/Shutterstock; 4: Jani Bryson/Istockphoto; 5l: Konstantin Chagin/Shutterstock; 5c: Anest/Shutterstock; 5b: Keattikorn/Shutterstock; 9: Catalina Mas Sebastián/Istockphoto; 10-11: Leonid_Tit /Shutterstock; 11c: Steve Collender/Shutterstock; 13c: Photos.com/Getty Images/Thinkstock; 13b: Jörg Drews/Istockphoto; 14-15: Image100/Photolibrary; 16: Daniel Schoenen/Shutterstock; 17: Eyecandy Images/Photolibrary; 21: Sheng Li/Reuters; 22: © J-P. Scherrer 2005; 24-25: Mike Jacoby/LaGrange Daily News/AP Photo; 25c: AlesVeluscek/Istockphoto; 27tl: Volodymyr Krasyuk/Shutterstock; 27tr: Ase/Shutterstock; 27cl: Zirconicusso/Shutterstock; Restyler/Shutterstock; 27cr: Brooke Fuller/Shutterstock; 27bl: Patty Orly/Shutterstock; Alexei Nikolaevich; 27br: Sashkin/Shutterstock; 28: Carolina K Smith MD/Fotolia; 29: Justin Sullivan/Getty Images News/Getty Images.

Q2AMedia Art Bank: 6–7, 8, 10, 12, 18, 19, 20, 23, 24.

12 11 10 9 8 7 **14 15 16/0**

Printed in the U.S.A. 40
First printing, September 2011

Table of Contents

Chapter 1

WHACK! A snowball lands perfectly on your friend's back. Just a few months ago, you welcomed a summer rain to cool you off as you played kickball in the heat. Now, in the cold of winter, that same water is frozen into flakes of snow that pack together nicely for wintertime fun with snowballs, igloos, and snowmen.

How can that same water that fell from the sky as rain over the summer now fall as cold, fluffy flakes in the winter months?

Snow can be a lot of fun, but what exactly is it? **Snow** is really a frozen form of water. The beautiful flakes you see begin to form when the air gets cold enough for water droplets inside clouds to turn into ice. Snow is one type of precipitation. **Precipitation** is any form of water that falls from clouds to Earth's surface. Rain is another type of precipitation.

SMART WORDS

snow a frozen form of water that falls from clouds to Earth's surface

precipitation any form of water that falls from clouds to Earth's surface

The Water Cycle

Rain and snow both begin as part of the water cycle. This is the never-ending movement of water on, above, and below Earth's surface. The same water goes through the water cycle over and over again. This means that the water you use today is the same water that first appeared on Earth billions of years ago!

There is no beginning or end to the water cycle. But you can start with evaporation and follow along in the diagram to see how water moves and changes.

1

SMART WORDS

evaporation the process in which water changes from a liquid to a gas, or water vapor

condensation the process in which water changes from a gas to a liquid

1 EVAPORATION

The sun heats water in rivers, lakes, and oceans, causing it to evaporate. In the process of **evaporation**, water changes from a liquid to a gas, or water vapor.

2 CONDENSATION

As water vapor rises high into the sky, it hits cool air. In the process of **condensation**, water changes from a gas back into a liquid.

3 PRECIPITATION

Tiny droplets of liquid water collect in clouds, and will eventually return to Earth's surface as raindrops or snowflakes.

Cloudy with a Chance of . . . ?

So what makes some precipitation fall as rain and some fall as snow? The temperature of the air!

Water is the only substance on Earth that can exist as a solid, liquid, or gas — and still be the same substance. Solid, liquid, and gas are the states of water. Water can undergo a **change of state** by gaining or losing heat energy — getting hotter or colder.

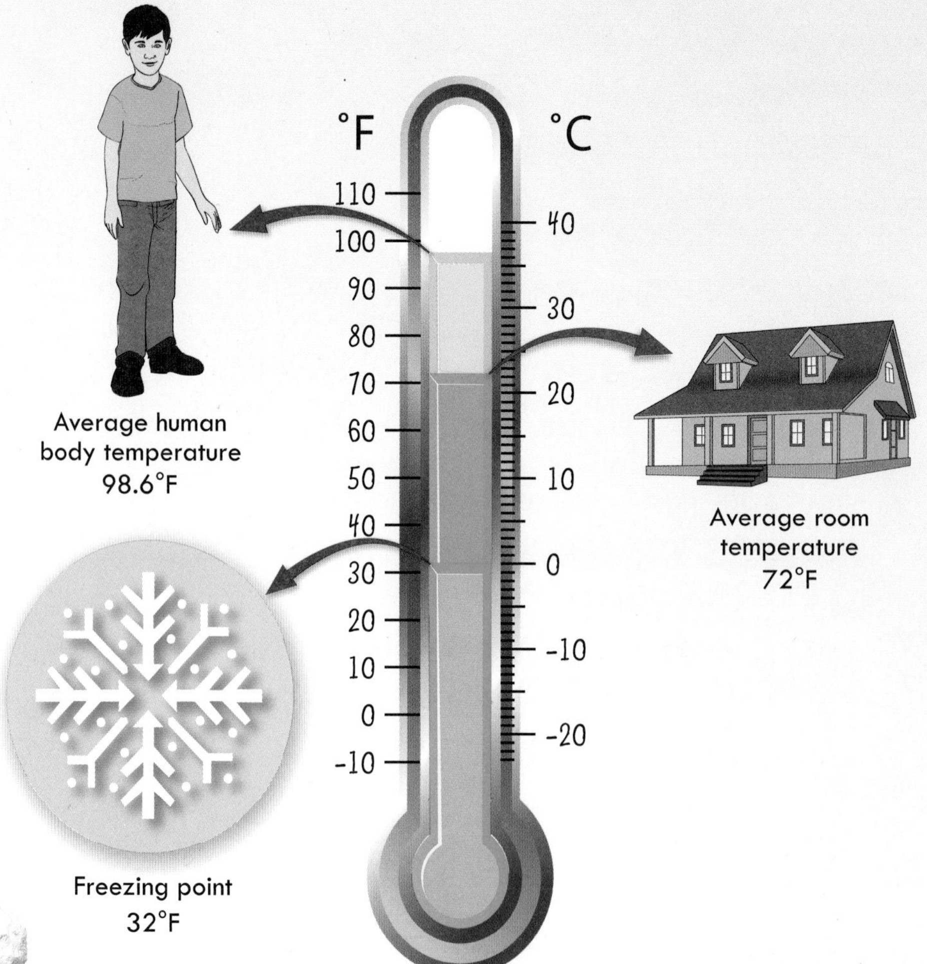

When liquid water loses heat energy, it changes into solid ice. This process is called **freezing**. The temperature at which water freezes, 32 degrees Fahrenheit (0 degrees Celsius), is called its freezing point.

Snow forms when temperatures are below water's freezing point. At such low temperatures, water becomes supercooled. It can change from water vapor (a gas), directly into a solid — or snow.

If you have ever held a snowflake in your hand, you probably noticed that it melted quickly. That is because your hand is warm. When the solid snowflake absorbs heat energy from your hand, it changes into a liquid. The process in which a solid changes into a liquid is called **melting**.

SMART WORDS

change of state the process in which matter changes from one state, or form, to another

freezing the process in which a liquid changes into a solid

melting the process in which a solid changes into a liquid

Snowflakes: No Two Alike?

The life of a snowflake begins when water vapor collects inside a cloud. With temperatures below freezing point, snow is formed out of crystals of ice. A **crystal** is a solid made up of particles that have a regular, repeating pattern.

For water droplets to form a crystal, they need a tiny particle in the air to grow on. As these small droplets collide and combine, a crystal pattern begins to form.

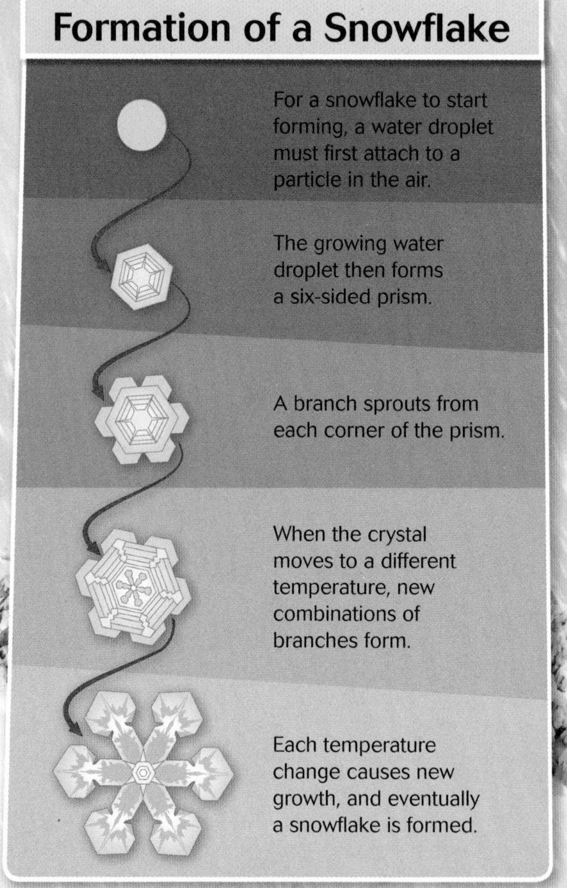

From a basic six-sided crystal, the snowflake begins to take its own unique shape. A branch sprouts out from each corner. Then, depending on the amount of moisture in the air and the temperature, new combinations of branches continue to form. A snowflake continues to grow and change as it falls through layers of air at different temperatures. Even a tiny change in temperature will affect how the crystal grows. As a result, no two snowflakes are alike!

Because of the way they form, every snowflake has a unique shape.

SMART WORD

crystal a solid made up of particles that have a regular, repeating pattern

Match each description with the correct Smart Word.

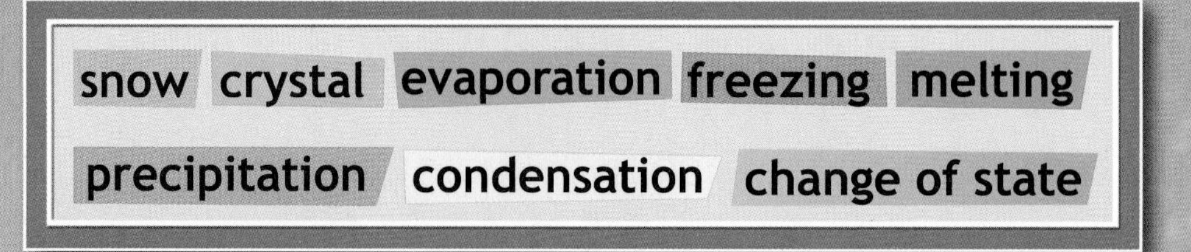

1. any form of water that falls from clouds to Earth's surface
2. a solid made up of particles arranged in a regular, repeating pattern
3. the process in which a liquid changes into a solid
4. any change from one form of matter to another
5. a frozen form of water that falls from clouds to Earth's surface as flakes
6. the process in which a solid changes into a liquid
7. the process in which a gas, or water vapor, changes into liquid drops of water
8. the process in which liquid water changes into a gas, or water vapor

Answers on page 32

Talk Like a Scientist

Explain where the water that forms snow comes from. Use your Smart Words.

SMART FACTS

Did You Know?

Snow looks white, but each snow crystal is actually clear. The way that the groups of crystals reflect light makes them look white.

That's Amazing!

Did you ever notice that many animals living in the polar regions have white coats? This helps them blend in with the white snow, making it easier for them to hunt prey and harder for predators to see them!

Incredible Fact

Penguins are well suited for life on the snow and ice. They have feathers and layers of fat to keep them warm. But to keep their eggs warm, penguin fathers hold the eggs in a special pouch on top of their feet!

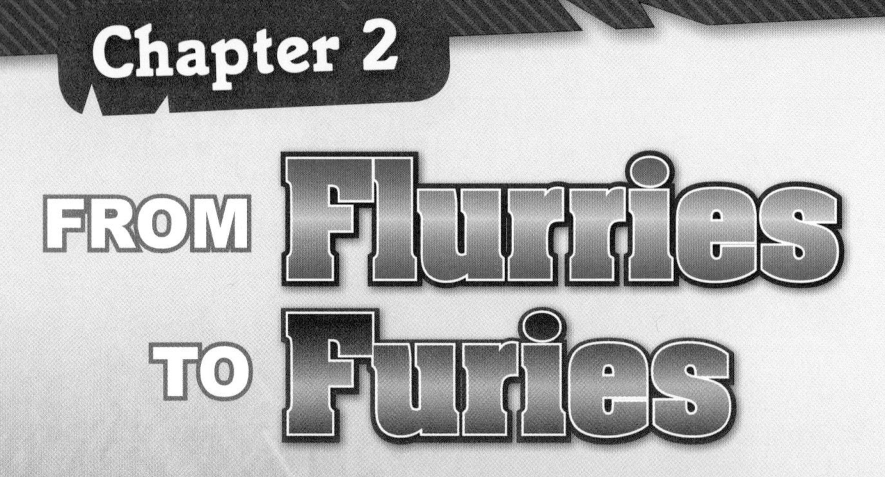

Chapter 2

FROM Flurries TO Furies

When a winter storm becomes severe, it might turn into a blizzard. It is not the amount of snow that makes a storm a blizzard. In fact, blizzard conditions can occur without any snow falling at all. A **blizzard** is a winter storm with winds that are at least 35 miles (56 kilometers) per hour and blowing snow. This may be snow that has already fallen to the ground. In addition, the distance you can see through the snow must be a quarter of a mile or less for at least three hours.

SMART WORDS

blizzard a winter storm with winds of at least 35 miles (56 kilometers) per hour and blowing snow that is either falling or already on the ground

snow squall a brief but heavy snowstorm along with gusty winds

A **snow squall** is a storm that might seem like a blizzard. During this type of storm, heavy snow and gusty winds occur for a short period of time. These storms may result in a heavy buildup of snow. Look at the chart to compare several forms of winter weather.

Types of Winter Weather

Snow flurries	Snow showers	Snow squalls	Blizzards
Light snow falls for a short period of time. No real buildup of snow occurs.	Light snow, mixed with bursts of heavy snow, falls for a brief period of time. Some snow may build up on the ground.	Heavy snow showers occur along with strong, gusty winds. A significant amount of snow may build up on the ground.	Falling snow or snow on the ground is blown around by winds over 35 miles (56 kilometers) per hour, reducing visibility for at least three hours.

Stirring Up a Blizzard

Imagine standing on the bottom of a swimming pool. You can feel the weight of the water above you. In a way, you are always standing at the bottom of a pool — a pool of air. The weight of the air is known as **air pressure**.

Air pressure is not the same from place to place. Some regions have high pressure while others have low pressure. Air always flows from areas of high pressure to areas of low pressure. The movement of air is called **wind**.

Because there are great differences in air pressure when a blizzard forms, the winds are very strong.

With winds hammering at over 35 miles (56 kilometers) per hour, blizzards can cause serious damage to trees and property.

The high winds make the snow whip through the air. Sometimes this makes it impossible to see. When this happens, it is called a whiteout.

The strong winds of a blizzard can also make it feel colder than it really is. The difference between the actual temperature and how cold it feels because of the wind is known as the **wind chill factor**. A strong wind can make the temperature feel like it is about 35 degrees colder than it actually is.

SMART WORDS

air pressure the weight of the air at any particular point on Earth

wind the flow of air from a region of high pressure to a region of low pressure

wind chill factor the effect of lowering the temperature due to wind

How Much Snow?

Some places get a lot more snow than others, even if they are nearby. The depth of snow on the ground is called the **accumulation**. For example, places around large lakes can have uneven accumulations of snow.

The reason for this is that water can be warmer than nearby land. When cold, dry air flows over the warmer waters of a large lake, the air picks up moisture that can form **lake effect snow**. This can result in a large accumulation of snow on the side of the lake toward which the wind is blowing.

As cold, dry air passes over a warmer body of water, it picks up moisture that will freeze into snow.

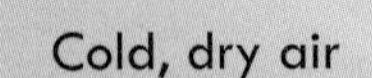

A different process is at work along some mountain regions. Moist air from nearby water is forced to flow upward when it reaches the mountain. As it rises, it cools and forms clouds. If temperatures are low enough, precipitation falls as **mountain effect snow**. By the time the air reaches the other side of the mountain, it has given up all the snow.

One side of a mountain may receive a large accumulation of snow while the other side gets none.

SMART WORDS

accumulation the buildup of a substance, such as snow

lake effect snow snow created when cold, dry air passes over a large, warm lake and picks up moisture

mountain effect snow snow created when moist air flows up a mountain, where it cools and forms snow

Use your SMART WORDS

Match each description with the correct Smart Word.

blizzard · air pressure · accumulation · mountain effect snow · wind · snow squall · wind chill factor · lake effect snow

1. I am a storm that has high winds and blowing snow that is either falling or already on the ground.
2. I form when cold, dry air picks up moisture by blowing over warmer water.
3. I am air that moves from a region of high pressure to a region of low pressure.
4. I am a brief storm with heavy snow.
5. I am the buildup of snow on the ground.
6. I am the weight of the air at any particular point on Earth.
7. I make you feel colder because of blowing winds.
8. I am snow created when moist air flows up a mountain, where it cools and forms snow.

Answers on page 32

Talk Like a Scientist

Write a short news report describing what causes lake effect snow. Use your Smart Words in your description.

SMART FACTS

Incredible Snow

As light as one snowflake may be, when many pile up they can be a disaster for roofs. In one extremely snowy season, a small region in Connecticut experienced roof collapses at a shopping plaza, an airport hangar, a church, and over 130 barns.

That's Amazing!

While some people are shoveling snow out of the way, others are piling it up into incredible snow structures. Some of the largest snow structures can be found at the Shenyang International Ice and Snow Festival in China, like this sculpture of the Daming Palace.

Did You Know?

The Blizzard of 1996 continues to be one of the worst storms ever experienced by the mid-Atlantic states. Even the government offices in Washington, D.C., had to shut down for nearly a week.

Chapter 3
Not Just Snow!

Imagine looking outside to discover that everything is covered by ice. How does ice form without snow? Sometimes in winter, a layer of warm air develops between two layers of cold air. As snow falls through the warm layer, it melts into rain. As it moves through the lower layer of cold air, the rain becomes very cold. This causes a type of storm known as an **ice storm**.

An ice storm can cover everything in its path with a thick coat of ice.

SMART WORD

ice storm a storm in which sleet or freezing rain causes the ground to be covered with ice

Ice storms can be caused by sleet or freezing rain. Both are caused by snow that has melted in the sky. Sleet refreezes before it hits the ground. Freezing rain doesn't refreeze until it hits the ground.

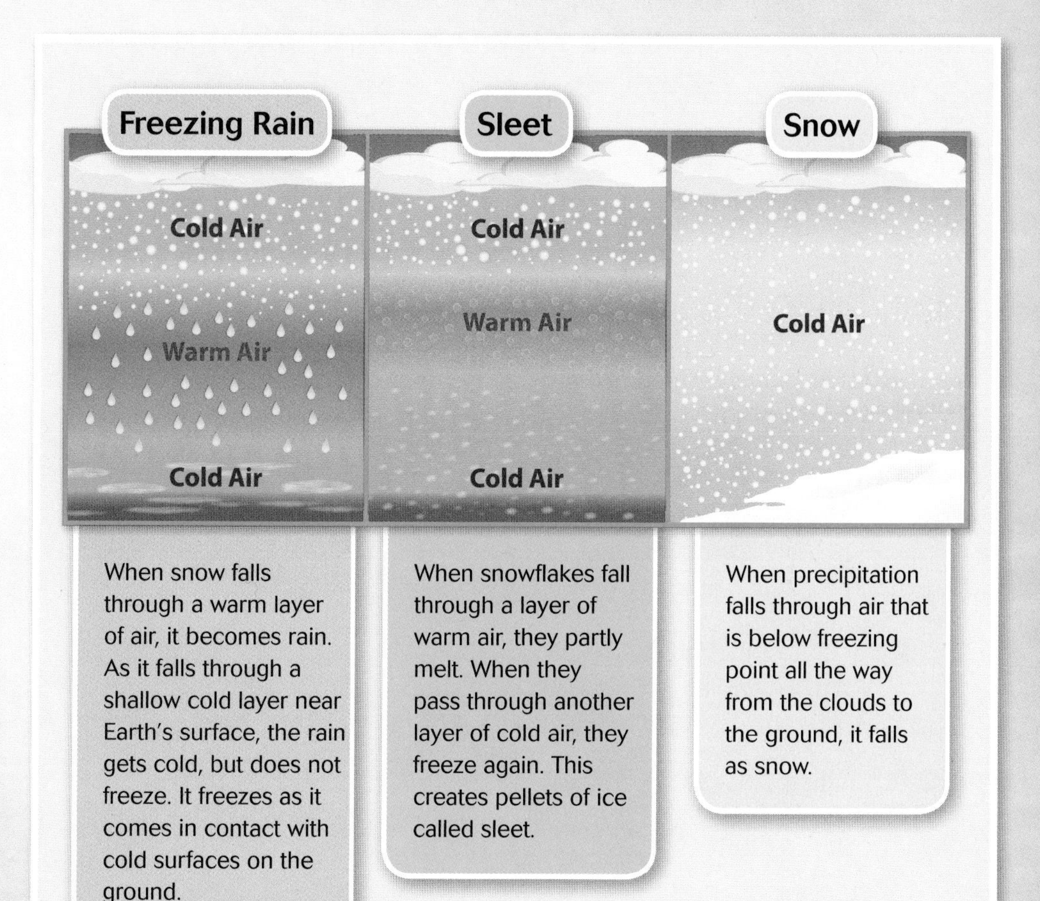

What Is Hail?

It is a warm summer day when dark clouds quickly fill the sky. You see lightning and hear thunder, and then large balls of ice are suddenly falling from the sky. What's going on?

The balls of ice are a frozen form of precipitation called **hail**. Hail forms inside a thundercloud. As the rain falls, strong upward winds push the rain higher in the cloud. Because the cloud is colder at the top, the rain freezes. The frozen rain can then fall to the ground as hail.

Sometimes hail can be as big as a baseball. That happens because the same rain can get pushed upward by the wind several times. Each time it gets pushed up, it gathers more moisture that adds another layer of frozen ice. The speed of the upward wind determines how big the hail will get. The faster the wind is, the larger the hail can grow.

Hail that is this large can damage cars, property, and crops.

SMART WORD

hail frozen precipitation that forms when rain is pushed upward in a thundercloud

Ready for a Snow Day

Have you ever gone shopping right before a big storm? Lines at the grocery store are long as people stock up on food. Shovels are often sold out. People know when to prepare for winter weather because they listen to weather forecasts.

A winter storm **watch** indicates that winter weather, such as heavy snow, sleet, or freezing rain, is expected. The conditions will probably occur within the next 12 to 36 hours. When a watch is issued, it is time to gather supplies, such as food, water, and flashlights.

WATCH	WARNING	ADVISORY
Winter weather conditions are expected within the next 12 to 36 hours.	A severe winter storm is occurring or likely to occur, and is considered to be dangerous.	A winter storm is occurring or is likely to occur, but is not life threatening.

When you see weather alerts on your television, you should pay attention and start making necessary preparations.

When a storm is occurring, imminent, or likely to occur, and it poses a threat to life or property, a watch is changed to a **warning**. A warning is usually issued for a smaller region than a watch, and for a more definite period of time. When a warning is issued, stay indoors.

A winter weather **advisory** is somewhat in between a watch and a warning. The winter storm is occurring, imminent, or likely to occur, but the conditions should not be life threatening.

SMART WORDS

watch an alert indicating that winter storm conditions are expected, probably within the next 12 to 36 hours

warning an alert indicating that a winter storm is occurring, imminent, or likely to occur and it poses a threat to life or property

advisory an alert indicating that a winter storm is occurring, imminent, or likely to occur, but is not life threatening

Match each description with the correct Smart Word.

hail   ice storm   watch
warning   advisory

1. an alert indicating that a winter storm is occurring, imminent, or likely to occur, but is not life threatening
2. a storm in which sleet or freezing rain causes the ground to be covered in ice
3. an alert indicating that winter storm conditions are expected within the next 12 to 36 hours
4. frozen precipitation that forms inside a thundercloud
5. an alert indicating that a winter storm is occurring, imminent, or likely to occur and it poses a threat to life or property

Answers on page 32

Talk Like a Scientist

A severe winter storm is quickly approaching. You need to provide a weather alert. Explain how you would decide between an advisory, a watch, or a warning. Use your Smart Words.

SMART FACTS

How Can That Be?

When liquid water changes to ice, it releases heat energy. Farmers sometimes use that heat energy to keep crops warm during cold weather. They spray water on the crops so that it can turn to ice. The ice actually seals heat into the crops, protecting them from the cold.

That's Amazing!

Adding salt to water lowers its freezing point. That means that is has to be colder for the water to freeze. Salt is often spread on roadways and sidewalks to prevent ice from forming.

Did You Know?

Some hail is like a baseball dropped from an airplane flying through the sky. The hail can reach speeds of up to 120 miles (193 kilometers) per hour. That can do a lot of damage!

Glossary

accumulation the buildup of a substance, such as snow

advisory an alert indicating that a winter storm is occurring, imminent, or likely to occur, but is not life threatening

air pressure the weight of the air at any particular point on Earth

blizzard a winter storm with winds of at least 35 miles (56 kilometers) per hour and blowing snow that is either falling or already on the ground

change of state the process in which matter changes from one state, or form, to another

condensation the process in which water changes from a gas to a liquid

crystal a solid made up of particles that have a regular, repeating pattern

evaporation the process in which water changes from a liquid to a gas, or water vapor

freezing the process in which a liquid changes into a solid

hail frozen precipitation that forms when rain is pushed upward in a thundercloud

ice storm a storm in which sleet or freezing rain causes the ground to be covered with ice

lake effect snow snow created when cold, dry air passes over a large, warm lake and picks up moisture

melting the process in which a solid changes into a liquid

mountain effect snow snow created when moist air flows up a mountain, where it cools and forms snow

precipitation any form of water that falls from clouds to Earth's surface

snow a frozen form of water that falls from clouds to Earth's surface

snow squall a brief but heavy snowstorm along with gusty winds

warning an alert indicating that a winter storm is occurring, imminent, or likely to occur and it poses a threat to life or property

watch an alert indicating that winter storm conditions are expected, probably within the next 12 to 36 hours

wind the flow of air from a region of high pressure to a region of low pressure

wind chill factor the effect of lowering the temperature due to wind

Index

SMART WORDS Answer Key

Page 12
1. precipitation, 2. crystal, 3. freezing, 4. change of state, 5. snow, 6. melting, 7. condensation, 8. evaporation

Page 20
1. blizzard, 2. lake effect snow, 3. wind, 4. snow squall, 5. accumulation, 6. air pressure, 7. wind chill factor, 8. mountain effect snow

Page 28
1. advisory, 2. ice storm, 3. watch, 4. hail, 5. warning